Other Books by Thom S. Rainer

ANATOMY OF A
REVIVED
CHURCH

SEVEN FINDINGS OF HOW CONGREGATIONS AVOIDED DEATH

1

2

3

4

5

6

7

THOM S. RAINER

ANATOMY OF A REVIVED CHURCH

SEVEN FINDINGS OF HOW CONGREGATIONS AVOIDED DEATH

THOM S. RAINER

ISBN 978-1-948022-17-0

Published by Rainer Publishing
www.rainerpublishing.com
Spring Hill, TN

To
"The Boys"
Sam Rainer
Art Rainer
Jess Rainer
Incredible Sons
Models of Christlike Character
My Best Friends

And Always
to
Nellie Jo
of Course

Contents

Before the Autopsy

"You were too late."

It was an unusual statement from a man I had never met. Indeed, I had to pause for clarification. "Excuse me?" I asked.

"You were too late."

There were those words again. I had not mis-heard them. The expression on his face clearly told me he was not joking. He was serious. Dead serious.

Others at the conference wanted to speak with me. Though I was tempted to begin a conversation with the next person, I could not leave the man with the stern expression without an explanation.

"So, where was I too late?" I asked him.

"It was your book," he said. "*Autopsy of a Deceased*

Church. I read the book in one sitting. But it was too late."

I waited.

"My church had already died. We closed the doors just a few months before I read your book," he said quietly. "Why didn't you write something sooner? Why couldn't we have made some changes before we had no choice but to die? I just don't understand."

And then I saw it. At first, I thought his eyes were just irritated. But those were tears. Real tears.

He was not angry. He was hurting. Deeply hurting. His church had closed. I would learn it was the church where he was married and where his two daughters married. It was the church he attended faithfully. It was the church he loved deeply.

Now it was closed. But he chose the word "died" first. The man was deeply grieving a death.

I asked him to stick around. I wanted to hear his story and his church's story, but I could not be rude to the others who were waiting. I was grateful he waited on me. We talked for almost an hour after the conference ended.

I heard his story.

Churches That Choose to Die

In May 2005 Alan Deutschman wrote a cover story for *Fast Company*. The article was simply but profoundly titled, "Change or Die." The responses were so voluminous, Deutschman expanded his work into a full book by the same title. It was released in early 2007.

There were two major reasons the article and the book had such eager audiences. First, the research for his topic was meticulous and thorough. Second, the results were breathtaking. His central thesis was both profound and disturbing. If given a choice between life and death, most people and leaders choose death if life requires substantive changes.

Reflect on that previous sentence a moment. Most people choose death rather than change.

Even if they have the path to live, the resources to live, and the choice to live, they choose death rather than make the necessary changes.

Deutschman pointed to some disturbing realities that confirmed such an astounding claim. For example, among 600,000 patients who undergo heart bypass surgery each year, a significant number of them can be restored to full health with lifestyle changes in their eating and exercise habits. But 90 percent do not make any changes. They are choosing to die.

Such choices of death, Deutschman tells us, are not limited to personal health. He points to many leaders of organizations who know what changes they need to lead for the organization to live or even thrive. Yet they do not make those changes, and the organization dies.

Here is the disturbing reality in all of these examples. Individuals and organizations do not lack the resources, knowledge, and information to survive. They simply do not choose to make the changes that are clear and available. When confronted with the choice to change or die, they choose to die.

No one knows for certain how many churches close their doors in the United States each year, but it's probably safe to say the number is at least 7,000, and that number is growing. Twenty churches are closing their doors every single day. Most of them did not have to die. Most of them chose to die.

I know. My words sound harsh. But reality can be a tough taskmaster. As I will explain in greater detail in the next chapter, we cannot begin to change until we accept reality.

Here is another bit of sobering reality. More churches are marching toward the precipitous path of death every year. Ten years ago, about 10 percent of all churches were declining so rapidly we deemed them terminal or near terminal. Today, 19 percent of all churches in America are in that category.

Stated another way, the number of churches near death has grown from 35,000 to 66,000 in ten years.

Change or die.

A few years ago, I saw this reality up close. A church near death asked me to speak to their remnant of members. As I entered the deteriorating facility, I saw the signs of death everywhere. The church sign was covered by weeds. You could not see the name of the church from the road. I decided not to take a men's room break when I opened the door to the restroom. It was filthy beyond words.

In one of the rooms off the sanctuary was the old upright piano that a member had donated to get a tax write-off. But no one had ever played it; the church was just a better dumping ground than the landfill.

But more than the facilities were the faces of the members. They were defeated. A couple of them were angry. They had given up hope, or at least they saw me as their last hope.

I vaguely remember saying a few words about change when I was interrupted by a lady almost all the way in the back. There were fewer than a dozen people left in the church, but she had to sit in the last pew.

"What about the screens?" she asked.

"The screens?" I asked with bewilderment.

"Yeah," she said with growing indignation. "Will we have to have words on the screen instead of our hymnals if we make these changes? You're not supposed to have screens in a church!" The other heads nodded in affirmation.

I wrapped up my presentation quickly. The church members thought it was more important to have dusty hymnals than to be a gospel presence in their community. They had already made their decision. There was no need for me to waste my breath further. They had chosen to die rather than change.

Change or die.

There are thousands of them. In fact, if you include all the declining churches in America, three out of four churches are change-or-die churches. Some are declining rapidly toward death. Others are declining slowly but must decide to change before their condition worsens.

Change-or-die churches. Robert's church was one of them.

They chose to die.

The Sad But Common Story

Robert was the name of the man at the conference. His was the church that died. By the time we met after the conference, he had regained his composure. He wanted to talk. And though I am an introvert by nature, I wanted to hear his story. So I mostly listened.

"Our church was founded in 1961," he began. "I took a job in the community when I was in my twenties. I joined the church right away and stayed with it until it died."

Robert paused for a moment. I could tell his

articulation of those last three words took him by surprise: "until it died." It still seemed surreal to him that his church no longer existed.

"I was already engaged when I moved to town, so I wanted to make sure my wife was okay with the church. She loved it. In fact, she loved it so much, she made the decision to have our wedding there. The people were so loving. We just wanted to build our lives around the church in our neighborhood."

That was the first time I heard the church was located in a specific neighborhood. I asked Robert if he lived near the church.

"Oh yeah, we bought a house only two blocks away," he responded. "We would walk to church unless the weather was bad."

I then asked him if he still had a home in that same neighborhood. I could have predicted his response.

"No, we moved out of the neighborhood after living there for almost twenty-five years," he told me.

Why?

"Well, the homes in the neighborhood began to decline in value. There were some other changes as well. We just didn't feel good about staying there," he said with a bit of hesitation.

I could tell he was uncomfortable with my question, so I decided to approach it differently later in the conversation. I moved to a happier discussion.

"Tell me about your daughters," I said. For the first time in the few minutes I had known Robert, I saw a smile on his face.

"My girls are incredible," he exclaimed. "God blessed us with Sarah and Michelle. We raised them in the church. Sarah married a guy from the church, and Michelle married a guy she met a college. They are such a joy! Even more, the two girls have given us five grandchildren."

Now I really understood that joy!

I thought I knew where Robert would take the conversation. At least on this one occasion, I was on target.

"I guess the saddest thing about the church was when the two families left the church," he began. "They didn't leave at one time, but it was pretty close together. They bought homes in different parts of town. To be fair, a lot of the young families left in just a short period. We got to the point where we didn't really have anything for the young families. We got different youth ministers to solve the problem, but that didn't change things much. And we finally called a young pastor with three kids, but he didn't stay long either. It was like every time we thought we had a solution, it didn't work."

I didn't have the heart to tell Robert I had seen the "silver bullet" solution fail time and time again. Instead, I tried to ease back into the conversation about the changing community around the church

"So," I asked, "did a lot of the members still live in the neighborhood right before the church closed?"

"No, not really," he responded. "In fact, only one person, one of our widows, lived in the neighborhood for the last five years the church was open. You've got to understand, the community was changing fast. The people moving in really weren't like us. Our members weren't racists or anything. But most of the people we know, most of our families, moved out. You understand?"

Yes. Unfortunately, I did understand.

The Pre-Autopsy

Robert changed the conversation quickly. He wanted to get back to talking about the book I wrote several years ago, *Autopsy of a Deceased Church*. I wrote the book after talking to a number of people like Robert. In every case, I got to hear stories about churches that died. I got to hear the common themes about these deceased churches. I thus, in some ways, got to perform an autopsy of deceased churches.

My initial understanding of Robert's claim that I was too late was not exactly clear. He was not saying he wished he had read the book earlier. Instead, he said I needed to write a book before a church dies, before an autopsy is performed.

I found humor in his suggestion that I write a prequel called *The Pre-Autopsy*. I understood what he meant, though. He wanted a resource on death prevention. In essence, he wanted a book on church revitalization. I initially dismissed the idea since there were already a wealth of books and resources on the topic.

But the more I spoke with Robert, the more I realized he was probably pointing me in a different direction. He understood we have an abundance of material, resources, consultants, and coaches to provide solutions for revitalization. That is not the key issue.

Instead, *the key issue is why church members and leaders choose not to change even when the solutions seem to be staring them in their collective faces.* In fact, Robert could articulate well the wrong choices his church made. What he could not explain is why the church continued down the path of wrong choices.

They chose tradition over change.

They chose comfort over change.

They chose preferences over change.

Ultimately, they chose death over change.

A Necessary Caveat

I do not want to assume you know my assumptions. Instead, I want you to hear clearly the necessary change of which I speak is not biblical change. There are foundational, unchangeable issues.

- The Bible is the Word of God.
- Jesus died for sinners.
- He defeated death with His resurrection from the grave.
- Christ is the only way of salvation.
- God is the Father, the Son, and the Holy Spirit.
- Eternity is a reality.

There are many other unchangeable truths, but I want you to hear clearly that this book about change is not about compromise of biblical truth. To be clear, any human-centered change is headed for failure. True change in our congregations must be rooted in the truths of the Bible, saturated in prayer, and empowered by Him alone.

Yet, there is so much we can change. Let me state it more emphatically. There is so much we *must* change.

To the Roberts in Our Churches

With a few exceptions, I write for church leaders, particularly pastors. They are my primary audience. While I do not exclude pastors and other church leaders from my audience, this book is also for the Roberts in our churches. For you church members, Robert told me to get a message to you.

"Would you consider writing something to us church members before there is a need for an autopsy?" he asked. "Don't just tell us *what* needs to change. Don't just tell us *how* to change. Tell us *why* we need to change. Yeah, give us the tough news; we need to hear it. But also give us hope. Point us to a better future where our churches will *want* to go. Don't drag us there. Lead us there."

I could see it happening again. Robert was thinking about his deceased church. Even more, he was grieving about his church.

"I'm trying to find another church home, but it's tough. After nearly thirty years at one church, it's tough. I've gone through the stages of grief, and I'm not done grieving yet. But I'll tell you one thing, wherever God leads me to find a church home, I won't make the same mistakes. Perhaps God will use the death of my church to be the catalyst for other churches to live."

He already has, Robert. He already has.

Would you, church member, approach this book with prayer and discernment? Would you ask God how he might speak to you through the words you are about to read? Would you be willing to put aside personal preferences and desires so that your church may not just survive, but thrive? Would you take a moment to absorb some of the tough news and realities so you can see the hope of which I write?

The hope comes in the form of an anatomy. We have figuratively dissected hundreds of churches that have been on the path toward death. But they turned around. They revived. They did so in the face of facts and naysayers who told them it could not be done.

In its simplest form, these churches chose to live. I can anticipate what you're thinking. What church wouldn't choose to live? But remember the story of Robert's church. It chose to die.

Get ready to walk with us through the anatomy of churches that were revived because they chose to live. Get ready for the prequel to *Autopsy of a Deceased Church*, a prequel called *Anatomy of a Revived Church*.

These churches chose to live. The choice is as simple as it is profound.

Change or die.

And now, in God's power, the choice is yours.

Questions for Prayerful Consideration

1. How would you evaluate your church right now? Healthy? Not so healthy? Very sick? Dying? Why did you make that particular choice?
2. Why do you think about three out of four churches are declining today, and about one in five are dying?
3. Do you know of a church that has closed its doors? Why do you think these churches die?
4. As we look at "change or die" realities, name some areas we cannot consider changing.
5. What are the similarities between a person refusing to change health and lifestyle issues and a church refusing to change methods and programs?

Chapter 1

Anatomy Finding #1: Accepting Responsibility

"I learned it in anatomy."

Our family heard that sentence untold times from my oldest son, Sam, when he was in high school. He took a course in anatomy and was enthralled by it. Again and again, he would remind us of all the things he was learning in that course. It became such a redundant sentence that his two brothers would ask Sam every time he said something, "Did you learn that in anatomy?"

At times those three brothers could be a little tough on one another. I may or may not have contributed to the anatomy sarcasm.

But I got why Sam was fascinated by the course. It

dealt in detail with the bodily structure and organisms of humans and animals. You learned so much about the amazing makeup of God's creatures. You could see the component parts that explained the whole.

Anatomy can also be a good term to explain what we see when we analyze and dissect other things. Indeed, it is specifically helpful to understand congregational life and the life cycle of churches.

I have analyzed a lot of churches since I began this type of research back in the mid-1980s. I estimate I have examined the data, at least on the surface, of over 100,000 churches. These congregations taught me a lot, both good and bad.

By far, my most enjoyable research over the years has been analyzing churches that are alive and well after going down a path that seemed destined for death. I have called them "breakout churches," "turnaround churches," "revitalized churches," and "revived churches," to name a few.

But I have been inspired by people like Robert whom you met in the previous chapter. While he appreciated my book on church autopsies, he wanted to know how churches could avoid death. At least, that is what he wished had been available for his church before it was too late.

As I have considered similar requests and questions, I knew the task before me. I had to get into the world of the anatomy of churches, specifically those churches that were once headed toward death and now are alive and well. Such is the purpose of this book. In each chapter, I look from an anatomical perspective at what these revived churches did. I will examine the component parts that made up the whole of a revived congregation.

The first component boils down to the choice of blame and denial versus acceptance and responsibility. I have seen it hundreds, if not thousands, of times. Dying churches blame others. Revived churches accept responsibility. So who and what do dying churches blame? Here are a few of the culprits.

"It's the Other Church's Fault"

Their expressions were somber. Their body language was tense. I don't think they wanted to meet with me. A mutual friend arranged the meeting. He told the three church members at the table that I could help their church.

After five minutes, I doubted I could.

So tell me about your church, I began. I was not expecting a joyful response.

"We've got a problem," one lady began. Good, I thought. At least they recognize there is a problem.

"It's the megachurch in our town," she continued. Delete any positive thoughts I had to this point.

"Yeah," a man next to her spoke up. "It's sucking the life out of our church. We can't compete with their children's ministry and the smoke and loud noise of their worship services."

I was tempted to ask, "Smoke is the problem?" I refrained.

For nearly thirty minutes I listened to them complain and criticize another church. I heard nothing about their church investing in the community. I heard nothing about their responsibility to evangelize and to minister to others.

It was the other church's fault. That summed it all up.

I came prepared. I showed them a demographic map. There were over 17,000 people within three miles of the church. The percentage of unchurched was estimated to be 78 percent.

"Look, there are over 13,000 people within three miles of your church who don't go to church!" I exclaimed.

I waited for their response.

I wish I could say I was waiting with joyful expectation. I wasn't.

"Yeah," the other woman responded. "Probably the only place they will go is that megachurch that's stealing our members."

Sigh.

I left our meeting as soon I could get away.

"It's the Worship Style's Fault"

I wish I had a dime for every time a church member of a declining church concluded that worship style is the reason for their congregation's decline. Typically, the declining church is more traditional in worship style and their examples of growing churches are typically more contemporary in worship style.

The members and leaders of these churches usually conclude they are being faithful by their traditional worship style while the contemporary churches are headed down the path to perdition.

"We aren't going to compromise by doing away with our hymnals for loud music and smoke," a Baptist deacon declared to me.

There's that smoke thing again.

Here is a secret for most church members: Contemporary music is not the silver bullet for a turnaround. The real issue for the healthy contemporary churches is their desire to understand, minister, and reach their communities. It's called contextualization.

Some healthy churches are contemporary. Some are traditional. Some are liturgical.

Some unhealthy churches are contemporary. Or traditional. Or liturgical.

Worship style is neither a silver bullet nor an excuse.

If you're ready for your church to revive, dump the excuse of worship style.

"It's the Pastor's Fault"

I got fired as a church consultant.

Okay, that's a bit of hyperbole. The clearer way for me to say it is I never was retained as the church consultant for this church.

It began as an initial conversation between seven leaders from the church and me. We were sitting around a large table. It was an ordinary request. The church was in a twelve-year decline and, almost in desperation, decided to seek outside help. I was the consultant they called.

"What do you see as the primary reason for the decline?" I asked after a few conversational formalities.

It took a few moments, but the oldest person at the table spoke. "Well," he began cautiously, "I don't like to throw anyone under the bus, but it basically comes down to our pastor."

I asked him to elaborate.

He responded, "The pastor came in and wanted to change a bunch of stuff, like the worship style. He didn't visit our members enough. And he sometimes preached too long."

Others nodded in affirmation.

After an extended discussion of the pastor problem, I opened my chart for them to see.

"Here are the names of the pastors for the past

fifteen years," I began. "There are five in all. I've learned that all five were either fired or pressured to leave. That's an average of one pastor termination every three years for fifteen years. You have a reputation in the community of being a 'preacher eater' church. With all respect, I don't think you have a pastor problem; I think you have a people problem."

I didn't get the consultation.

"It's the Denomination's Fault"

While denominational loyalty is waning, the real growth is in denominational blaming.

Of course, thousands of churches do not belong to a denomination, so they can't add this one to their list. But many are denominational. And many would place the responsibility at the feet of the organizations, leaders, and workers in their respective denomination.

The denomination's resources are inadequate.

We can't get a denominational worker to assist our church.

The denomination does not care about us little churches.

The denomination doesn't have all the free events they used to have.

You get the picture.

Many denominations began as an organization of churches of similar doctrinal beliefs and heritage. They often were a conduit to fund mission work around the nation and the world. They may have supported some seminaries or colleges.

But somewhere along the way, many church leaders saw denominations as their personal resource assistants. And many denominations did just that for a season. Then denominational loyalties started waning and the funds for these endeavors were cut significantly.

For many, it's now the denomination's fault.

"It's the Community's Fault"

This one used to surprise me. No more. I hear it with too much frequency.

Here is a conversation I heard a few months ago. I quote the pastor's words to the best of my recollection.

"This community is not like it was twelve years ago when I first came here," he began. "Our church was like a magnet to the people around us with our programs and ministries. We could announce something, and people would flood into our church."

The obvious question from me: What happened?

"Well, the community started changing," the pastor explained. "A lot of our members moved out, even though most of them kept coming to our church. But the people who moved in those houses were not like our church members. They weren't at all interested in our church," he explained.

"I don't understand it," he said. "We would welcome them if they came. And they must know we are here. You can't miss the big white columns out front."

"Perhaps," I said with trepidation, "your church might go into the community instead of expecting them to come to you."

"Nah," he said with a hint of indignation. "They're not interested in us. If this church dies, it will be because of the community."

Yep. It's the community's fault.

"It's the Demographic's Fault"

This path of blame can go in several directions. One is to blame the perceived scarcity of unchurched people. I have heard countless times how there are so many churches in a community and how everyone who wants a church home has already found one. The tone is futility: We can never reach anyone because there is no one left to reach.

I've been working with churches over three decades. I have *never* been in a community that has no one to reach. Never. Ever.

A corollary of this blame game is simply to say the population base is too small. There are just not that many people in the area.

To be fair, I have been in rural communities with a small population. I get that. Churches in those communities will likely never be large. Still, there are always people to be reached.

One of the most rewarding conversations I had recently was with a pastor whose church was in an area with a population of 400 within a five-mile radius. That's sparse! The fatalists in the church warned him he would do well if he could lead the church to hold its attendance average of forty-five.

The pastor was not deterred. He led the church to minister to the population in many creative ways. The rural community got the message. The church cares. The members care. Five years later, the church attendance is 95. Almost one out of every four people living in that rural community attend that church on a given Sunday.

It's not the demographic's fault.

Anatomy of Accepted Responsibility

Change or die.

Church leaders and members who refuse to accept their God-given responsibility to reach and minister both inside and outside the walls of the church buildings are on a clear path to decline and likely death.

But church leaders and members who embrace the reality of the Great Commission and Great Commandment for their lives will be a part of churches that don't just survive and live but instead thrive and grow.

When we did our anatomical study of the churches that moved from a path of decline and death to one of life and growth, we saw a commonality early in the turnaround, indeed before the turnaround became visible.

Usually a few leaders determined in God's power that they would stop blaming others and other situations. They would take responsibility for their own obedience and lack of obedience. The blame game, they discovered, does nothing but increase frustration.

A pastor in New Jersey decided to set aside five hours a week to connect with people in the community who were not a part of the church. Soon one other person joined him, then eight more followed. Those ten people became an outward focus and evangelistic force that invaded their community with gospel conversations and ministry.

Three women at a non-denominational church in northern California stopped blaming the pastor, staff, and lazy church members for the decline of their church. Instead, they began to pray fervently for God's power in their congregation. They met twice a month and used an app every day of the week to remind them to pray together at a specific time.

The church, four years later, is beginning to show signs of reviving. It has been slow and arduous, but it sure beats blaming others.

Members of a church in Florida watched helplessly as their church declined for eleven consecutive years. The path toward death seemed inevitable. Pastors who were supposed to be the silver bullet came and left in one to three years. Frustrations were high, and the blame game was pervasive.

Five of the members, all senior adults, became weary of the decline and blame syndrome, and they began to pray for God to direct them in a positive way. They all began to find places in the community to care and love for people they never knew. They became the hands, feet, and mouth of Jesus.

Three years later, the church began to turn positively. No, there has not been dramatic growth, but the signs of life are evident. Hope has replaced fear. Obedience has replaced blame.

One member summed it well: "If you had told me three years ago we would begin to have hope in this church, I would have said you were crazy or either a miracle had taken place. I believe a miracle has really happened."

You see, it's not others' fault. It's not the fault of the situation in which your church finds itself. In our anatomy of revived churches, we saw blame transform to words of hope, encouragement, ministry, and possibility.

Anatomy finding number one is clear: Church leaders and members accepted responsibility. In God's power they moved forward.

The blaming of others came to an abrupt and glorious halt.

Questions for Prayerful Consideration

1. Read Acts 6:1–7. How did the church in Jerusalem move from blame to obedience?
2. Again, look at Acts 6:1–7, particularly verse 7. What were the immediate results of their obedience?
3. What are some common ways you have seen blame expressed in churches?
4. What does it mean when we say the church members and leaders "accepted responsibility"?
5. Why do you think this finding in the anatomy of a revived church is mentioned first among the others?

Chapter 2

Anatomy Finding #2: Overcoming the Traps of Traditions

L EON.
It's one of our favorite Christmas traditions. Allow me to explain.

For the entirety of the lives of our three sons, one of our Christmas decorations was four porcelain blocks, each with a different letter on it. For example, one of the blocks had an "L" on each of its six sides. Another had an "E." Then another had an "O." Finally, a block had an "N" on each of its six sides.

The Christmas decoration was meant to be displayed as NOEL. But our three sons, even at early ages, took a strange delight in rearranging the letters that usually sat on our fireplace mantel. You would rarely see NOEL. You might see LONE or ONEL, but the most common was LEON.

LEON, for reasons unknown to me, became one of our Christmas traditions.

Then tragedy struck.

One of the grandkids got hold of one of the blocks. Most grandkids have the spiritual gift of destruction. This one was no exception. The block broke into three pieces.

The tradition ended with an abrupt crash.

At least it ended until next Christmas.

My wife, Nellie Jo, could not bear to see the looks of disappointment on her sons' three faces with the departure on LEON. I am sure they were devastated beyond measure. By the next Christmas, the broken block had been Gorilla Glued to health.

LEON was back. The tradition endured.

Was the Rainer family a group of recalcitrant sinners because we enjoyed our tradition? Should we have donned sackcloths laden with ashes for our fondness of this ongoing fun in our home.

Of course not.

Tradition is not evil. Indeed, traditions can carry generations of positive messages and legacies.

Traditions are not inherently evil. Where traditions become a fixation or obsession, they often become issues of idolatry. They become more important than sharing the gospel message, reaching people, serving the community, and making changes to make a difference.

It is in those times churches become trapped by traditions. Constancy is perceived to be godly and change evil.

In essence, the tradition becomes an object of worship.

A Traditional Top Ten

A few years ago, I conducted an extensive survey asking what church leaders and members viewed as the most problematic and divisive traditions in their churches. Most of the responses were not a surprise, but a couple did seem to come out of left field. The top three are connected to the corporate worship services. Indeed, there are a lot of emotional connections to the way we've always conducted our worship services.

#1: Worship Music and Style

The worship wars are waning in many churches, but they are far from being over. Indeed, when church members began to fight and gripe about the well-worn traditional versus contemporary music issues, defining the terms can be elusive. I know one church where the key issue was the over-dependence of music from the 1990s. That era represented traditional music to some of the members. But many church members are still convinced the era of God's music was the 1950s and 1960s.

It can be discouraging. Some churches cling more tightly to their music preferences than they do their Bibles.

#2: Order of Worship Service

The deacons in the church really did have a meeting about firing the pastor because he moved the offertory from the middle of the service to the end of the service.

I'm serious.

I was asked to intervene before the fateful meeting. When I inquired about the source of conflict, I laughed at their response. My laughter was not meant to be disrespectful. I really did think they were joking.

"So, the deacons are meeting about firing the pastor?" I asked. "And the offense is he moved the offertory to the end of the service?" I asked again. The chairman of the deacons answered in the affirmative to both questions. He would admit the pastor only committed this unpardonable sin one time because of other changes in the service that day.

But it did seem to be an unpardonable sin to him. "You just don't put the offertory at the end," he told me in complete seriousness. I avoided the temptation to confirm that the Apostle Paul indeed prescribed middle-of-the service offertories. I'm not so certain I was right to show constraint.

The good news is that the deacons decided not to vote in that meeting for dismissal, but to give the pastor a stern warning about his abominations.

The bad news is the pastor left the church as soon as another called, about five months later. The worst news is that, seven years later, the church is about to close its doors.

#3: Times of Worship Services

For years, the 11:00 Sunday morning worship service was perceived by many to be the sacred hour of worship, the *only* holy hour. The reality is the 11:00 a.m. time is a tradition that had merit when it was first conceived. Though its origins are not certain, the best evidence is that the service time was started in a mostly agrarian society. The farmers had to get the chores done, so the later morning time gave them enough cushion to milk the cows and feed the farm animals.

But some churches have become fixated on other times. "Don't take my 8:00 a.m. service time away," one elderly church member told me in a church consultation. The fact that she referred to the service time as *my service time* spoke volumes.

#4: The Role of the Pastor

Pastors simply need three characteristics to satisfy all their church members: omniscience; omnipresence, and omnipotence. It's basic for you pastors. You just have to know everything, be everywhere, and do everything. That's it.

Expectations of pastors by many church members are beyond unreasonable, and most of them fall in the trap of traditions. Too many church members see the pastor as the person who *does* all the ministry, instead of the one who equips others do to the work of ministry (Ephesians 4:11–12).

The consequence of this unbiblical view of the role of the pastor is a tradition of unreasonable expectations. The pastor can never satisfy all the members. Pastors can't be everywhere and have mind-reading abilities.

Two common sentences we hear in churches holding on to this tradition are: "That's what we pay the pastor to do" and "We pay your salary."

Both sentences are unbiblical, insensitive, and downright mean.

#5: The Role and Functions of Committees

At their inception, most committees served a healthy function. They were created for a real need at a specific time with clear functions, but over time, many committees met to meet. They lost their purpose. They continued to function because that's the way they've always done it.

It is a sadly amusing sight to sit in on a committee that has no clear purpose. I have done so countless times in my role as a church consultant. Not only will they meet with no purpose, they will fill the time slotted for them to meet. If it's a ninety-minute slot, they will meet for the full ninety minutes. It's an excruciating waste of time and life.

Even worse, some committees attract the control freaks in the church. They try to make the committee their base of power and influence. It's hard to kill a committee because some of these people will lose their sense of identity and control if the committee goes away.

Even more disheartening, unnecessary and traditional committees replace the time members could spend in ministry and more meaningful use of their resources. Countless churches fall into the trap of tradition with their committee structures. Some churches have more committees than they do conversions.

#6: Ministry and Programs

The conversation was telling, if not sad.

I was interviewing several leaders in the church as a part of a church consultation. This one meeting was with the chairman of the elders. He had stated unequivocally that the greatest need in the church was a stronger evangelistic effort. I liked this man. His heart was good, and his diagnosis seem spot on.

Then came my fateful question: Why do you think evangelism is so anemic in this church?

His response was a program. It was an old program that proved useful over three decades ago but did not meet the context of today. Because the program worked years ago, he assumed it would be effective today.

I knew the program well. It was created for a specific context at a specific time. I knew of no church where it was effective today. Times had changed. Contexts had changed. Yes, there was still a great need for effective evangelism in the church. But it was not a specific program whose effectiveness had waned thirty years earlier.

The elder's solution to the problem was not Great Commission obedience as much as it was the tradition of a program.

#7: Church Buildings

The battle was not resolved except by government action.

The church building had no visibility. It was so well hidden, many locals in the community did not know it existed.

The church needed to move.

And here was the issue. The church *could* move. It had the money. It had the land. It had a location that was still in the community but much more visible and accessible.

But the majority did not want to move. In many ways, I understand. Some of the members had been married in the old building. Some were baptized there. Others had funerals for loved ones in the sanctuary.

I understand, but they still needed to move.

Finally, the state government made them move. The state needed the property for a new highway that would cut right through the existing building. The church fought it at first but, of course, they lost the court battle.

And now the church has to move. It was one of those rare cases where an external force made the church change for its good.

But most churches will hold to the traditions of their building. And some will not let go until the doors close forever.

#8: Specific Rooms in the Church

One church raised money for a gym to reach the community. Ten years later, a new tradition was in place that only allowed members in the gym. Those community members were just messing up the place.

Another church held to the tradition that an expensive parlor could only be used for weddings. On the average the room was used three times a year.

And then there are the countless traditions connected to sanctuaries and worship centers. We will gladly have a welcome center with coffee, but don't you dare bring that coffee into the sanctuary. Signs everywhere indicate those with food or drinks in the sanctuary will be shot on sight. Okay, I speak with a bit of hyperbole, but you get the picture. These are traditions that can hinder a church greatly.

#9: Business Meetings

There seems to be a direct relationship between frequency of business meetings and divisiveness in churches. It seems like the tradition of the monthly business meeting attracts the malcontents and naysayers in the church. They see the routine of the monthly meeting as a platform to air their grievances publicly.

I believe the monthly business meeting began as an effort with good intentions. But somewhere along the way it morphed into a tradition of conflict and contentiousness.

#10: Staff Positions

I had not thought of this issue as an entrenched tradition in churches, but it made the final spot of the top ten in my survey. One pastor shared with me how he almost lost his job when he moved a staff member's title from minister of education to pastor of discipleship. In some churches, the staff positions themselves become a tradition. At times, the church staff are the ones propping up the tradition.

Traditions abound in many churches. Some of the traditions are traps, but let's look at a church that moved from these traditions to greater health.

Anatomy of a Church That Overcame the Trap of Traditions

It began with prayer.

Specifically, the church set aside twenty-four hours of uninterrupted prayer at the church facilities. At least three people were present at all times—two people praying in separate rooms and a third person present for security purposes.

The church of about 160 in worship attendance had around 100 people participate in twenty-four hours of prayers. Consistent. Persistent. Uninterrupted.

Each participating member committed to pray through a prayer guide for one hour. The oldest participant, ninety-two years young, took the 2 a.m. to 3 a.m. time slot. She wanted to be an example for others. Her part of the story is telling: "I wasn't sure I could pray and stay awake for an hour, but the time flew," she told us.

Was there any one part of the hour that stood out to her?

"Yes," she responded quickly. "There was one question about traditions in the churches. It asked if we were holding on to anything for our own comfort, routines, or preferences. I heard from a lot of church members about that question. It became an eye opener!"

What happened?

"Well," she said with utmost seriousness. "We began to look at all the things we do in the church. Many of us realized we were holding on to some traditions for own preferences. In fact, some of the things we did actually hurt our ability to reach into the community. We began to let go, tradition by tradition."

Our anatomy of this church revealed the process was not painless nor free of conflict. But the anatomy did reveal God honored the open hands and open hearts of the members. The church stopped worshiping the unholy trinity of me, myself, and I.

The church changed. The church changed for the better. The members' focus went from inward to outward. Slowly but steadily people from the community started visiting. The church turned around. The growth was not spectacular, but it reversed a slow decline of over twenty years.

The congregation became a revived church. God did an incredible work in a church many had deemed hopeless, including a number of its members.

The members let go of the idols of tradition. The focus was no longer "the way we've always done it." Instead, the members opened their hearts to what God wanted them to do. It was not always easy, but God blessed it.

The amazing thing about this story is that it completely defied human expectations, and it was something any church could do. Any church could do it if many of the members could let go of the unnecessary traditions. When we forsake idols, God begins to do a great work among us.

Questions for Prayerful Consideration

1. How can a tradition in a church become an idol?
2. If someone were to look at your church from the outside, what are some of the traditions he or she would notice within a few weeks? Name several.
3. How many of those traditions reflect more of the preferences of church members than any truly God-centered purposes?
4. Which of those traditions mean the most to you personally?
5. How do traditions become traps that lead a church to decline?

Chapter 3

Anatomy Finding #3:
Expanding the Scorecard

I took my grandson, Joshua, to his soccer game. He had one request of me: Keep the score.

He was young, so there was no scoreboard and there was (supposedly) no one keeping score.

Joshua did not like that rule. In fact, most of the parents and players seemed to be circumventing the rule one way or another. A lot of us were keeping score.

To be clear, Joshua understood his granddad's competitive nature, and he knew I would be keeping score. But Joshua wanted to know the score too. He asked me with all sincerity, "Why would we play a game when you don't keep score?"

I even heard him assure his teammates he could

tell them the score since his granddad was at the game. About every ten minutes he would look to me on the sideline to get an update on the score.

I get it. We can go overboard on scorekeeping and tracking numbers. We can make sports so competitive we lose sight of the fun they were intended to be. And we can obsess so much over numbers in the church that we forget our real purposes.

Indeed, I can remember the days when many churches were overly focused on numbers. I can remember when numerical church growth was the measure of a church's worth in the eyes of many. I am glad those days are fading.

But the pendulum has swung too far. Those who do any kind of numerical tracking are sometimes shamed for their misplaced focus. Such a shift has been to the detriment of many churches. Failure to count has often resulted in failed accountability.

And that brings us to the issues of revived churches and an amazing discovery in our anatomical process. Churches that have revitalized are counting. They have a scorecard, and many of them expanded the scorecard.

The Expanded Scorecard

Let's get clarity on this issue. The leaders of these revived churches weren't sitting around a table and had a moment of reality when they suddenly decided to start counting. No, they intentionally decided to change what the church was doing. They decided to move from an inward focus to an outward focus. And when they asked if their changes were effective, one way they answered that question was by counting.

What was fascinating about these revived churches is *how* and *what* they decided to count. Most of them had at least two metrics they followed closely. Some of them had as many as four or five. Let's look at the most common areas where revitalized churches counted.

Worship Attendance as a Scorecard

Worship attendance has become the most common metric among churches today. For most churches, worship attendance includes everyone who attends a primary worship service in a given week. The number includes children who were present but not physically in the worship service. The number, if done accurately, only counts each person once. So, the praise group singer who was in two services the same Sunday is only counted once. I get it. We can become too technical with how we count and what we don't count. My point is to share methodologies without obsessing over them.

But let's return to the issue of the revitalized church and the scorecard. Did these churches just decide to start counting worship attendance one day and revitalize shortly thereafter?

Not exactly.

Let me take you to a church in the southwest United States that decided to dream again. The leaders knew something was askew in the congregation. They saw the slow erosion of participation and motivation. And many of the leaders saw the attendance numbers for worship services each week. But few of them picked up on trends.

They decided to call me and my consulting group. I admired their love for their church. I admired their courage to call on a consultant. They knew something was wrong, and they were sought help. But they had trouble articulating their problems. Their perspective was more instinctive than a deep dive into the data and trends in the church.

So, I did something quite basic. I counted.

I took their average weekly worship attendance for ten years. I showed the basic numbers on a graph. The decline was not steep, but its impact over ten years was, in the words of one of the elders, "breathtaking." I can confirm his word choice. I actually heard a few gasps when they saw the worship attendance trends.

To the credit of the leaders, they neither panicked nor surrendered. For certain, they needed a few days to absorb the bad news.

Then something great began to happen. The church leaders began to dream again about what the church could do. They began to take seriously their mission to the community around them. They made intentional efforts to move from an inward focus to an outward focus.

I could see the change taking place before my eyes. Before my six-month assignment with the church was over, I was confident the church was moving in the right direction. My confidence was confirmed over the next two years.

By the way, how did the church stay on track? Did they use any metrics to make certain they would not return to apathy and malaise?

They did indeed. They followed their worship attendance trends carefully. The leaders reasoned that worship attendance would be a good indicator if the community was responding to their newly restored outward focus.

Note what they did *not* do. They did not say they had to increase attendance. They did not say they had to have a numerical turnaround. Instead, they dreamed again and reached into their community.

But they counted as a point of accountability. If fewer people attended worship services, then the efforts to reach the community were not effective. They would prayerfully make the necessary changes.

Did you get the nuanced difference? They did not count for number's sake. They counted to make certain they were on track. They counted for accountability.

As we studied revitalized churches, we saw more and more of them take numbers seriously. They saw the importance of the scorecard. Worship attendance was their primary scorecard, but it was not their only scorecard.

Financial Giving as a Scorecard

If your church publicizes any figures in the bulletin or newsletter, then the two most likely figures are worship attendance and financial giving. The giving scorecard can make people more nervous than any other (if you are behind budget). The giving scorecard can make people apathetic as well (if you are ahead of budget).

Some churches do not publish their giving numbers. It's understandable. I've heard from many pastors who undergo regular scrutiny with budget numbers. Fall behind just a little bit and people start making negative assumptions.

Not every church makes giving figures available to everyone. However, tracking your finances is critically important. Churches that do not pay attention to giving are vulnerable to creating a culture in which financial mismanagement can happen. Financial accountability requires proper tracking of revenue and expenses.

Additionally, giving trends can become leading indicators. Many people will stop giving before they stop volunteering or stop attending, especially when they are struggling spiritually. While there are numerous approaches to encouraging members to better stewardship, here are three key ways we have seen churches have significant success in increasing member giving.

First, have a systematic process for thanking first-time givers. One church in North Carolina saw a significant uptick in giving when they began to thank first-time givers systematically. They send a thank-you note and a book on biblical money management. They report that more of these first-time givers become regular givers, and their giving goes up over time.

Second, tie the money to the mission. An established church in Tennessee uses the offertory to remind people of why they give. Almost every single offertory is a time to showcase a ministry, with the pastor reminding the members, "This is why you give to God's work." This connection is particularly critical for the younger generations: Gen X, the Millennials, and Gen Z.

Third, thank generous members for their gifts. We heard from a pastor recently about his approach. He does not know the specific gifts of the members, but the financial assistant in the church gives him a list of the top 25 givers. He makes a point of taking them to lunch or coffee and thanking them. He tells them he does not know the specific amount they give, but he is aware they are generous givers. After the pastor got to all 25 givers over an eight-month period, the giving of those families increased by over 40%, and the total giving of the church increased by 25%. Generous givers to non-profits are thanked regularly. Sometimes generous givers in churches don't know if anyone even cares they are giving.

The Group Ministry Scorecard

Over seven of the ten revitalized churches made certain they tracked attendance in groups. It was part of the process of accountability to stay on the right track.

James is a pastor in Wisconsin. His church is a classic revived church. Like so many of the declining churches, this church experienced a gradual decline for many years, only to see the decline worsen the past few years.

He had been pastor at the church for twelve years. The gradual decline began before he arrived, but the pace did not stop under his leadership. "The church had declined from its peak attendance of 260 to 210 when I arrived," James told us. "Over the next seven years, the decline was gradual, but the attendance had dropped to 160. Then, it's almost like we woke up one morning and attendance hit below 100 on a Sunday in the fall. That's our 'good' attendance season."

"We were concerned," he said, "very concerned."

So the church began a revitalization effort. They got serious about obedience to the Great Commission.

Did they have a scorecard?

While James was not familiar with scorecard terminology, he readily affirms they followed two metrics closely and carefully to make certain they were on track. They followed their worship attendance and their community group attendance.

"We changed the name from Sunday school to community groups several years ago because a lot of our guests thought Sunday school was for children only," he told us.

When the church got serious about revitalization, one of the smart things they did was find out where they were seeing the most fruit. They found that those who stayed with the church in the decline were most likely to be a part of a community group.

"Over two-thirds of our losses were worship-only attendees," James told us. "Those who stayed were in community groups. Those groups were our sticky factor."

The church would also discover that the most generous and habitual givers were in community groups. And if someone in the church was involved in a ministry, he or she was inevitably in a community group.

"We saw how important the groups were to hold on to people during our decline," he emphasized. "We knew they would be important in our revitalization as well."

So, this church had a second scorecard. Groups were vitally important in the health of the church, so they tracked weekly attendance in the groups.

While watching attendance trends in the community groups was not the reason for the turnaround, it was an important scorecard they kept to monitor the turnaround.

The decline in the church has stopped. Growth is not dramatic, but it is steady and incremental. And the pastor and key leaders watch the trends in community groups.

They know it's just that important.

Scorecard for Conversions

Here is a question with an obvious answer: Do you think it's important for churches to be reaching people in their communities with the gospel?

Of course you do.

Here is another question: Is your church monitoring and watching closely the number of people who become followers of Christ? Do you know how many people God converted through the ministries of your church last year? Five years ago?

Over one-half of the revived churches we studied made a transition. They began including conversions as part of their scorecard. Different churches call them different names: conversions, baptisms, professions of faith, etc. But what most of them are measuring and following are the numbers of people who became followers of Christ through the ministries of the church and also became involved and connected with that church.

Frankly, I am amazed at the number of church leaders who do not know how many people their churches have reached with the gospel. If we think the gospel is important, if we think telling people about Jesus is important, if we believe Jesus is the only way of salvation, shouldn't we know how many people we are reaching?

Again, let me make some points perfectly clear.

We do not count for bragging rights. We do not count for number's sake. We do not count to see how good we are. We count for accountability. We count for obedience.

The scorecard is not necessarily a formal instrument we have to manage every day. For many churches, it is not an instrument at all. It is simply a way of keeping our priorities in front of us. It is about making the main things the main things.

As a reminder, here is what we found in the anatomy of the revived churches. Over half of them are now tracking conversion in their churches. Almost none of them were doing so before they committed to becoming a revived church.

It's simple, but it's profound.

The Ministry Scorecard

While over one-half of the revived churches kept expanded scorecards for worship attendance, group attendance, and conversions, fewer than one-third of the churches monitored their members' involvement in ministry. Still, I think it's important to note that three of ten of these churches kept this scorecard one way or another. None of them were doing so before the revitalization began.

So, what does it look like to have a ministry scorecard? Because we have to ask that question likely explains why so few churches monitor this important metric. It is fairly easy to measure worship attendance, conversions, and group attendance, but ministry-involvement measurement can be tricky.

Jenny serves as administrative director of a revived church. She was tasked to measure ministry involvement in her church, so she decided to keep it simple. "I spend about two hours a quarter keeping this metric," she told us, "and I keep it basic. I go through all the ministries of the church and write the names of the members who are involved in those ministries. I only count a person once, even if they are in more than one ministry. Then I add all the names. That's it. That's all I do."

Four times a year Jenny provides a single number to other leaders in the church. She has noticed that the church leaders have become more intentional about encouraging and moving people toward ministry involvement. "Since we began counting two years ago," she said, "we have only had one quarter where the number declined. But it was amazing to see how many leaders responded when they got the news. It's a form of accountability, and it really works!"

The Expanded Scorecard for Accountability, Not Obsession

I can say for certainty I did not expect to find a resurgence of scorecards in our anatomy of revived churches. But it makes sense. These churches knew they had to do things differently than before, so scorecards let them know how they were doing.

These tools, mostly simple and informal, are the tools of accountability. The church leaders of revived churches are not obsessed with them. But they do use them with diligence and discipline.

Indeed, it was encouraging to see how the church leaders responded to the metrics. If worship attendance was down over a consistent period, they asked hard questions of themselves. If group attendance declined, they would emphasize groups more. If conversions were not taking place, they would become even more intentionally evangelistic. If ministry involvement did not increase, they would seek to get more members involved.

What was amazing in this facet of the anatomy was not only to see their desire to measure what matters but to see their expanding of the scorecard to three to four different metrics.

As I reviewed this issue of the expanded scorecard, I realized what was taking place. These leaders of revived churches were doing their best to determine if they were really making disciples. Disciples gather for worship. Disciples come together in community. Disciples reach others with the gospel. Disciples are involved in ministry.

It is that awareness that gives me great hope. Revived churches are not about making much of numbers. They are about making much of God by being makers of disciples. In the final analysis of this anatomy, that's what matters.

Questions for Prayerful Consideration

1. What is the difference practically between being obsessed with metrics and with using metrics as a means of accountability?
2. Most churches track worship attendance. Why do most congregations embrace this measure?
3. Why would revived churches be more likely to have an expanded scorecard compared to other churches?
4. Why do relatively few churches have a scorecard for ministry involvement?
5. Why do you think this finding surfaced in the anatomy of revived churches?

Chapter 4

Anatomy Finding #4: Committing to Powerful Prayer

I have yet to see a sustained church revitalization that was not undergirded by a powerful movement of prayer.

Please read the first sentence again.

It is categorical. It is imperative. It is a priority.

We have seen churches turn around for a brief season with a new methodology or a new emphasis. We have seen some churches reverse their negative trends briefly with a new pastor or dynamic staff member. But we have yet to see a sustained church revitalization that was not undergirded by a powerful movement of prayer.

Perry Mason was a legal drama series that ran for

nine seasons from 1957 to 1966. Perry Mason, ably portrayed by Raymond Burr, played the part of a defense attorney who won almost every one of his cases.

While his winning percentage was not believable, what was more unbelievable was how he got his client acquitted. Mason would call the real guilty person to the stand and, somehow, get him or her to confess their crime under questioning. It happened almost every show. You knew the outcome, but the show's long run attests to its winning formula.

What Mason was able to do, at least as a television attorney, was to go below the surface and discover the issues no one was expecting. To mix the characters of fictitious illustrations, he was to the legal world what Sherlock Holmes was to the detective world. Both men could always see something beneath the surface.

When we conducted our anatomies of revived churches, it was rare that church leaders told us the revitalization began with prayer. They would often point to some of methodological matters I discuss elsewhere in this book. But then we dug more deeply. We sometimes asked if anything preceded the measurable revitalization. On other occasions, we asked specific questions about prayer. Inevitably, any question that sought to get at least one layer beneath surface issues yielded the same result. Prayer preceded and sustained revitalization.

Of course, we theologically know the power of prayer. That is to say, we believe it but don't always practice it. The tyranny of the urgent replaces the priorities of God. We are reminded that even Jesus had to chastise His disciples to pray in His moment of great need: "So, couldn't you stay awake with me one hour? Stay awake and pray, so that you won't enter into temptation. The spirit is willing, but the flesh is weak" (Matthew 26:40-41).

Our anatomy found that prayer was present and powerful in the revived church. Let's see how prayer manifests itself as we dig a bit below the surface.

The Principle of the Few

In every church I've served, I have been blessed to know a prayer warrior. Terminology is important here. A prayer warrior is a person who not only believes in the power of prayer but who also seeks to mobilize others to fight in the battle of spiritual warfare with him or her.

The prayer warrior in St. Petersburg was Lillian. She was energetic, outspoken, and motivated to get people involved in prayer. I loved her spunk and tenacity.

In Birmingham her name was Aulene. She was quieter and preferred to work behind the scenes.

Aulene worked as hard as any church member I've ever known.

In Nashville, the prayer warrior is Paul. He has a gregarious and warm personality that makes people want to be around him. It helps that he works hard to remember names of both church members and guests.

All of these prayer warriors have something in common: They usually only have a few people working alongside them to pray for people in the church and ministries of the church.

When Paul assumed the servant leadership role of prayer in our church in the Nashville area, I gave him a few words of encouragement. I let him know that he should not be surprised if only a few joined him in the ministry of intercessory prayer. Like Jesus's disciples who prioritized sleep over prayer, church members often are caught up in the busyness of life. Slowing down to pray does not seem urgent. Slowing down to pray in an intercessory prayer ministry in a church certainly becomes a low priority.

In our anatomy of revived churches, the power of prayer was evident, but it was not pervasive. To the contrary, most of the revived church leaders would point to a few who were the true prayer warriors in the church.

The principle is clear. Prayer is a prerequisite for revitalization; it is also a byproduct of it. In most cases, prayer in the church resides in the ministries of only a few faithful members.

But God is able and willing to use those few to be His instruments for revitalization.

We saw it again and again.

The big danger is succumbing to the suggestion that low numbers equals failure. In almost every church revitalization, prayer was the instrument God used, but He honored the consistent and persistent prayers.

For those of you seeking to lead a revitalization, let me exhort you. First, if you don't know the prayer warriors in your church, find them. Second, if you can't find them, start asking people in the church to help you find those who have a passion for prayer. Third, encourage those prayer warriors.

It is likely your prayer warriors have moments of discouragement. Here is a conversation I had with a prayer warrior named Sally in a consultation a couple of years ago.

I asked her what she thought the greatest need in the church was. Sally responded succinctly, "Prayer." I asked her if she could expand upon her voluminous answer. "Why should I expand?" she asked with a bit of indignation. "Everyone should know how important prayer is."

She then expanded without my further prompting. "I just don't get it," Sally said forcefully. "I asked people to show up to pray and only two or three join me. Sometimes it's only me. Why don't church members understand we can't do anything apart from prayer. Well, I guess we can sin. It gets frustrating."

If you are leading a revitalization or desire to lead a revitalization, make certain you know your prayer warriors and encourage your prayer warriors. In the anatomy of every revitalization, we discovered the unsung heroes and heroines.

Every revitalization. Every. Single. One.

An Anatomy of Persistence

I'm glad I didn't give up. She said "no" three times.

"She" is now my wife of more than four decades. Nellie Jo was my high school sweetheart. But before that, she was no more than wishful thinking for me.

You see, I asked Nellie Jo for a date three times and got three negative responses. It took the persistence of the fourth plea before she relented. She became my girlfriend and then my wife. She became the mother of our three sons and grandmother of our eleven grandchildren.

I don't even want to imagine the path of my life had I given up early.

In our anatomy of revived churches, we did indeed go one layer deeper and discover the primacy of prayer in revitalization. But when we peeled back another layer, we discovered the persistency of prayer.

Prayer warriors did not give up when only a few showed up.

I met Ruth at a conference where I was speaking on the topic of revitalization. So, I was not able to do an anatomy of her church's turnaround. The story line, however, was common to the revitalizations we have studied.

Though most members in her church were not aware of her leadership in persistent prayer, a few did. And a few of those would join her at church at 5:30 a.m. on Tuesday mornings.

"I felt like our church was headed toward death," she recalled. "It wasn't just the attendance numbers. We had not had a baptism in over three years. The spirit in worship services was dead. You could see it on the faces of the members. There was a real despondency in our church."

Ruth believed in the power of prayer. In fact, she had trouble understanding why more members were not turning to God in desperate prayer. "We would say we were praying for real sick and dying church members," she said. "But we wouldn't even talk about praying for our church that was sick and dying."

So, Ruth took the lead and began calling people to pray for the church. This pattern was also common in our anatomy of revitalized churches. One person began the call to prayer. It was not always one person, but many times it was.

One person. One person trusting God. One person believing in the power of prayer. One persistent person.

When Ruth began inviting people to join her for 5:30 a.m. prayer on Tuesday, she got a lot of polite but noncommittal responses. "I could tell they weren't interested," she said frankly. "No one was ugly about it. But they had no plans to pray for our church for thirty minutes on a Tuesday morning."

So, what did Ruth do?

"I started the prayer meeting anyway," she responded.

"At times, we had three or four of us," Ruth explained. "The biggest gathering we ever had was six. Most of the time it was just me and one or two others. Instead of giving up, I claimed the promise of Jesus in Matthew 18:20: 'Where two or three are gathered together in my name, I am there among them.'"

Here is a key we found in our anatomy. Not only was a small but powerful prayer movement active in every sustained revitalization, the movement of prayer rarely resulted in immediate fruit. Ruth's church was no exception.

"I wish I could tell you things turned around immediately," she told me. "But it seemed to be painfully slow at times. After over two years, though, we began to see some things change. It began with the attitude of our pastor and many members. Then it began to show itself in increased attendance. We even baptized someone three weeks in a row!"

Prayer. Persistent prayer.

To be clear, we are not suggesting that prayer, even persistent prayer, is God's guarantee for revitalization. It is up to Him and His timing.

But we have yet to uncover a sustained church revitalization where a small but powerful movement of prayer was not present.

What, then, can you do in your church if you desire to see prayer become a foundational movement for revitalization? In most of our anatomies, we found simple response to this question.

Most churches could name at least one person who actually sought the prayer warrior to lead the movement.

Seeking the Prayer Warrior

I was the prototypical discouraged pastor. I had tried all resources and programs I knew to try. At best, they were effective for a season. When they would run their typical course of interest, activity, and decline, I became even more discouraged.

Our church needed revitalization. To be clear,

I had never used the word "revitalization" before. When I was a pastor, it was not the buzzword it is today. Regardless, our church need revitalization.

I have been blessed to study spiritual awakenings in my seminary training. I even took a full doctoral seminar on the topic. While the older historical spiritual awakenings did fascinate me, a more recent awakening by historical standards caught my interest more than others.

It was called the Asbury Revival. Its origins are traced to a chapel service at Asbury College on February 3, 1970. It was a movement of confession. It was a movement of evangelism. It was a movement of restoration. Above all, it was a movement of prayer. If I have piqued your interest, read the little classic book *One Divine Moment* by Robert Coleman.

Prayer was central in all the spiritual awakenings. In each of those divine movements, God not only revived Christians, He revitalized churches.

I had that basic knowledge as I was serving as the pastor of a struggling church. I knew prayer was central and foundational if we were to have a true and lasting turnaround. But I needed one or more people to lead that effort in the church. How would God raise up the prayer warriors for our church?

I did something profound. I asked the members of the church.

Instead of waiting and wondering who would lead

a ministry of prayer in our church, I asked from the pulpit on a Sunday morning. I simply asked if God might be moving in the heart of someone to lead a ministry of prayer. I guess I called out the called.

By the time I got home, I received a phone call. It was Frances Mason. "Pastor," she said, "God wants me to be a prayer warrior."

I was both excited and relieved. I was excited because someone responded so quickly. I was relieved because it was Frances. I knew and loved Frances. She was the lone senior adult on the search committee that brought me to the church. She had demonstrated her love for my family and me repeatedly. I trusted her.

Frances was persistent. She would get people to pray for the church and for me at a designated time every day. She would simply tell them to pause and pray for one minute. That's it. She would remind them again and again. If she got discouraged with anemic responses, I didn't see it.

My point is simple. I asked for someone to step out and lead a ministry of prayers. If I had known the word then, I would have asked them to lead a prayer ministry for revitalization. Though I didn't know the nomenclature of revitalization, God began revitalizing the church anyway.

Prayer. Powerful persistent prayer.

When God Revives a Church

Our anatomy of revived churches was clear and persuasive. It is God who revitalizes churches. If we truly want to see His work in our churches, we must turn to Him in prayer.

The anatomy further revealed that God has been pleased to turn churches around when only a few people in the church are committed to pray for revitalization. One of more of those people tend not only to be consistent in their prayer lives, they are persistent as well. They don't give up. If they become discouraged, it is only for a season.

If you are seeking immediate application to the principle of powerful prayer in your church, begin praying God will provide a prayer warrior. Even more, ask the members in the church if God might be moving in their lives to lead a ministry of prayer for revitalization.

We have seen again and again in our anatomy of revitalized churches that every sustained church revitalization is undergirded by a powerful movement of prayer.

Every. Single. One.

It's just that important.

Questions for Prayerful Consideration

1. Many unsuccessful church revitalizations are marked by a ministry of prayer that was abandoned. Why do you think some churches give up on prayer ministries?
2. Why do we often wrongly equate successful ministries, specifically prayer ministries, with numerical success?
3. What are some characteristics of persistence in a prayer ministry?
4. In the literature of church revitalization, prayer is rarely given prominent focus. Why is that the case?
5. What are some examples of how a church prayer ministry might take place?

Chapter 5

Anatomy Finding #5: Dealing with Toxins

I told my parents I despised cigarettes. I am not sure what age I was when I first realized the harmful effects of cigarettes. Indeed, I grew up as a young child watching cigarette commercials. One of those commercials featured several physicians touting their favorite brand of cigarettes.

By the time I was a twenty-something, the deadly nature of tobacco products was increasingly becoming known. Warnings were on the cigarette packs and advertisements. Tobacco was deadly, a toxin.

I loved my parents dearly. Both were smokers from their teenage years. They were addicted, fully addicted. Breaking the addiction was not easy. In fact, despite a few efforts, they never succeeded.

I didn't want to blame my parents. I didn't want to heap more guilt upon them. So I blamed the cigarettes. And in one moment of deep emotion and concern for my mom and dad, I said through tears, "I hate cigarettes!"

Both of my parents died of the toxins. Dad died of cancer. Mom died after a fall with a weakened bone structure due to smoking. They never got to see all their grandchildren. They never got to see any of their grandchildren grow up.

Toxins are deadly.

Toxins can enter the human body in several ways. Smoking causes the toxin nicotine to enter the body. Both illegal drugs and addiction to prescription drugs are sources of toxins. The list of potential toxins to the human body is long. In all cases, the toxins are bad, often deadly.

Church toxins are deadly too.

Indeed, in our anatomy of revived churches, toxins were a recurring theme. It was usually one church member. On rare occasions, it was more than one. In all cases, the church member was toxic. He or she was a major disrupter of church unity and Great Commission focus.

In all the revived churches with a toxic member, the renewal did not take place until the negative member departed.

Easier said than done.

The Pain of Doing Something

Kicking the can down the road. It is common metaphor in leadership literature. It simply means putting off difficult actions today, thinking you can handle them in the future. Why do so many of us put off the painful tasks?

The obvious answer is that the task is painful. The very act of doing something inflicts pain on ourselves and others. Who wants pain?

Another reason is that we think things will get better on their own. Somehow, rather mysteriously, the problem will go away if we do nothing. Not only does the pain not go away, but the problem usually gets worse.

And yet another unspoken reason is fear of the toxic member and his or her allies. Fear that they will cause more trouble. Fear that they will leave with other members. Fear that people will withhold their financial gifts. Fear that they may force the pastor out.

Cliff is a pastor in Southern California. In his three years, the church had declined from 225 in worship attendance to 110. In other words, the church is half its size of just three years earlier. Cliff knew the problem within six months of his tenure. There was a toxic member in the church: Greg.

It did not take much discernment to see the problem. Whether it was constant criticisms, behind-the-scenes gossip, or open opposition in business meetings, Greg was consistently at the forefront of the problem.

So, what did Cliff do? He kicked the can down the road.

"I thought I could win him over at first," Cliff told me. "When that didn't work, I just ignored him, thinking the problem would go away if he didn't get my attention."

Neither strategy worked. Now, one-half of the active attenders are gone. And you can guess who left. It was largely the healthier and more unifying church members. So, now the church is not only half its former size, those who remain have supported or tolerated the toxicity.

The problem does not go away. It gets worse.

By the way, Cliff's church is obviously not the story of a revived church. It is the story of a dying church. In fact, in my last conversation with Cliff, he told me the church would probably close within in a year.

Greg is still there.

In the revived churches, the leaders confronted the problem and the problem makers. It was indeed painful. But the alternative never works.

Let's look at some healthy ways revived churches dealt with toxic church members.

Making Certain of the Toxicity

Toxic members are rare.

Read that sentence again. Slowly. Carefully.

Of the millions of people who attend church and who are members of churches, only a small number are toxic.

Indeed, it is possible your church does not have a toxic member. I have consulted with hundreds of toxic-free churches.

The problem, of course, is that it only takes one toxic member to destroy a church. Toxicity is a poison. If it is not addressed, it will eventually destroy the church. Thankfully, we learned much from leaders of revived churches on dealing with toxicity. Here are three of those lessons.

Lesson #1: A Critic Is Not the Same Thing as a Toxic Member

Every church has critics. Every single one. A critic disagrees with you, or they disagree with others in the church. A critic does not like some aspect of the church's ministry. But disagreement does not equal toxicity.

Brandon is a pastor in Arkansas. He learned early in his ministry about the differences between critics and toxic members. "It was not right on my part to label critics as toxic members," he told us. "I am actually glad that I had to experience a toxic member early on. Unlike the critics, his jabs were unending. Everything he did undermined the unity of the church. He was not only outspoken; he was also venomous with his words. He made 'normal' critics look like teddy bears in comparison. But I learned the difference between critics and toxic members. Now I approach them differently."

Lesson #2: A Toxic Member Has a Pattern of Misbehavior

Critics come and go. Toxic members stay forever, or at least it seems so. Brad Waggoner, a friend and incredible leader, reminds other leaders to watch for patterns of behavior. We are all prone to be critics from time to time. We all do things we wish we hadn't done. We all say things we would like to take back. But those behaviors are not the norm for us.

A toxic member has a pattern of disruption, disunity, and negativity that is persistent, consistent, and intense. Watch for the longer-term patterns. That is where you will find the toxic members.

Lesson #3: Followers of Toxic Members Are Influenced by Them, but They Are Usually Willing to Follow Healthy Leadership over Time.

It can be tempting to categorize a group of church members as toxic. That, however, is a rare exception. Toxic members have strong personalities, and they can attract a following for a season. But those followers are not usually toxic themselves. In cases of toxicity, you are usually dealing with one person, a few at most.

The consistent theme is that toxic members are rare. Church leaders of reviving churches recognized that reality and did not jump to conclusions or make ill-informed judgments.

The Persistent Prayer Theme

If this book were a streaming video, I would tell you to rewind it to the previous chapter. Revived churches are prayerful churches. Indeed, none of the findings in the anatomy of revived churches is a standalone issue. They are all overlapping and interconnected.

Especially prayer.

At the risk of redundancy, let us be reminded of the primacy of prayer in revived churches. And let us never, ever think church turnaround is a human-powered endeavor. We are His instruments, but we aren't the power.

We saw God's power unleashed again and again in our anatomy of revived churches. And, again, we saw the efficacy of prayer in dealing with toxic church members.

Marvin, for example, was in his second year as pastor of a church with a toxic member. Mary, the toxic member, ran roughshod over the previous pastor until he left defeated and unemployed. She was doing the same with Marvin.

"I was scared to death," Marvin admitted. "I had heard how Mary treated my predecessor, and I could see it happening to me. It seemed like I had two choices. First, I could do nothing and watch the church continue to decline and watch me lose my job. Second, I could confront the situation and watch the church blow up and watch me lose my job. Well, I didn't like either alternative."

Marvin also admitted he turned to prayer in an act of desperation more than obedience. "I wish I could say I was this godly pastor who had a prayer life second to none. That's not the case. I have a long way to go."

But even though his prayers were acts of desperation, God honored the prayers of Marvin and the few he asked to join him.

"I asked four people I trusted to pray every day about this toxic situation," Marvin told us. "I really believe the five of us did not miss a day of prayer for a few months."

After about three months, Marvin and one other leader in the church decided to confront Mary. "I was shaking when the three of us got together," he shared with us. "But, when I started speaking, I could feel my courage growing. When Mary would yell back at me, I would listened calmly and then speak even more strongly about her actions."

No, Mary did not leave the meeting repentant. She was mad. But when she tried to make an issue over her "mistreatment," she found little sympathy. The more she tried to gather alliances to force out the pastor, the more she found how her support had dwindled to nothing. Mary left the church. The fall-out was minimal.

"I don't guess I should have been surprised, but I was," Marvin told us. "The power of prayer never ceases to amaze me. You could tell a difference by the next Sunday. It was a moment where we could truly see God turning our church around."

We concluded our church anatomy with Marvin with his four departing words: "Prayer is really amazing."

Yes, it is.

The Power of the Guiding Coalition

When my sons were children, Nellie Jo and I took them to an exhibit in a children's museum called "the dark tunnel." The concept was simple—a maze you had to navigate in total darkness. You had to feel the walls and the passageways because you cannot see a thing.

I took our two older boys in the tunnel one at a time with an admonition from my wife, "Don't you dare let them go. They are not to be alone in the tunnel."

Got it.

Our lives as Christians were never meant to be alone. "Lone Ranger" Christianity is an oxymoron.

The same principle applies in Christian leadership. We are not meant to be autocratic leaders, totally on our own, without input or support from others.

In the churches where the problem of the toxic member was addressed, we saw a consistent theme in our anatomy: Leaders did not try to deal with the issue on their own. They prayerfully sought the wisdom and collective efforts of others. As one pastor told us, "Trying to confront the problem of a toxic church member on your own is just plain stupid."

So much for mincing words.

The pastor is right. We saw that reality in our anatomy of revived churches. When the problem of a toxic member became an issue, these leaders sought both the wisdom and the alliances of other members in the church.

"My alliance to deal with the problem of Mary," Marvin told us, "was not big in number. But it included some of the godliest and most influential people in the church. Depending on how you define 'alliance,' the number included somewhere between eight and fourteen. I knew once I had their prayerful support, we might be able to confront the problem."

By "confronting the problem," Marvin, of course, means confronting Mary, the story we just shared. That brings us to the obvious but final issue of dealing with a toxic member: Don't just stand there, do something.

The Unavoidable Issue of Confrontation

Here is the simple but difficult truth we learned in our anatomy of revived churches: Most pastors and other church leaders had to confront a toxic member. To a person, each of those leaders spoke of both trepidation and concern for the church before they moved forward.

Most of the leaders with whom we spoke followed the guidelines of Matthew 18:15–17:

If your brother sins against you, go and rebuke him in private. If he listens to you, you have won your brother. But if he won't listen, take one or two others with you, so that by the testimony of two or three witnesses, every fact may be established. If he doesn't pay attention to them, tell the church. If he doesn't even pay attention to the church, let him be like a Gentile and tax collector to you.

Since we were speaking with leaders of revived churches, most of the confrontation stories ended well, though there was a period of pain. And the church began to heal after the departure of the toxic church members. The departure was a key factor in the revitalization of the church.

To be clear, however, not all the stories end so well. In the past two months I have spoken with pastors who confronted toxic church members just as the revived church leaders did. Two of them lost the battle and were forced out of the church.

But, if a toxic member is allowed to continue his or her pattern of negativity and disunity, the church will decline. It may die. While church leaders have no guarantee a confrontation will work as they hope, they do have a guarantee the church will continue a slide toward decline and likely death if nothing is done.

Dealing with toxic church members is exceedingly difficult. But not dealing with them assures decline will continue.

Questions for Prayerful Consideration

1. How does the word "toxin" describe the most negative of church members?
2. What are three considerations you should make before assuming and declaring a person is a toxic church member?
3. How can a church leader bring others to pray for the congregation that has a toxic church member?
4. How does the passage from Matthew 18 have application in today's churches that have to deal with toxic church members?
5. How does a guiding coalition help the leader deal with the problem of a toxic church member?

Chapter 6

Anatomy Finding #6: Seeking Silver Bullets No More

Silver bullets have a mythical history. In several pieces of literature, silver bullets are the magic ammunition to kill werewolves, vampires, and witches. The Lone Ranger used silver bullets in his gun. It was his symbol for justice, law, and order. He also thought silver bullets were more accurate than normal bullets.

Over the years, the concept of silver bullets became a solution that had singular, immediate, and often magical results. For example, for many, winning the lottery would be their silver bullet to happiness.

I have consulted with hundreds of churches over the past thirty years. I have interacted with countless church leaders. The silver bullet syndrome is alive and well in thousands of congregations. The silver bullet sentence typically begins with, "If only we had . . ." Then the church leader or member informs me of that one magical solution that would turn their church around.

Here me clearly. There are no silver bullets for churches in need of revitalization. There are no shortcuts. The challenge of such a turnaround is usually arduous and long term.

In our anatomy of revived churches, the results were 100 percent. No successful church revitalization depended on a silver bullet. None of the leaders and members were sitting around waiting for a magical solution to their church's plight.

Look at that previous paragraph. None of the churches held to the silver bullet theory. Not one. If these results were part of a medical study, the findings would be considered groundbreaking. There were no exceptions to the rule, an anomaly in anomaly in almost any research.

So, our findings could be considered groundbreaking for the world of local congregations. The anatomy of revived churches revealed clearly that if you depend on a silver bullet solution for revitalization, it is guaranteed *not* to happen. In the world of statistics, it is called an inverse relationship or a negative correlation. Do *this* (waiting on silver bullets to turn the church around) and *this* (the church will continue to decline) will happen.

In simple terms, the church leaders and members of revived churches took responsibility for the church's problems. They did not wait for some magical or mystical solution to address the issue. In God's power, they began to move forward in obedience. We heard a plethora of silver bullets. Five of them, however, were repeated again and again. Let's look at them in order of frequency.

The Pastor Silver Bullet

As of the writing of this chapter, this story is fairly recent. But I have been in similar conversations more times than I can remember. Though I may not recall the words precisely, the conversation went in this direction.

So, I asked the four gathered leaders to share with me what the challenges were with their church. The congregation had declined in attendance from 175 to 83 over the past ten years. The first man who spoke called himself, somewhat in jest, "part of the youth group at the church." He was seventy-two years old. I would learn later that two-thirds of the church was older than he.

"We need a young pastor," he said emphatically

and without hesitation. I asked him to elaborate. "Well, if we get a young pastor, he will get new young families for us. Our last pastor stayed too long. He was in his sixties when he left. You know you can't attract young families with an old pastor."

The only woman of the four gathered leaders jumped in: "It wasn't just his age," she insisted. "He didn't visit members enough. And he stopped going on outreach visits three years before he left. You can't expect a church to grow if the pastor is not visiting the members and doing outreach. I think he just gave up."

Before the conversation continued, I asked if the former pastor was forced out. One of the other men answered my question. He identified himself as the church treasurer. "Yes and no," he replied. "We told him we didn't have the money to pay his full salary. We had to cut it in half and cut out all his benefits. He told us he would leave when he heard that."

The conversation continued in this same direction. I have been in enough of these meetings to anticipate the answer to my question, but I asked them anyway.

"So," I asked, "how can Church Answers help you?"

I don't think they really all spoke at once, but it seemed that way.

"Find us a young pastor!" they said.

Do you get the picture of this silver bullet? The

pastor silver bullet is, by far, the most common we heard from church leaders seeking revitalization for their congregations.

They want a young pastor.

They want a pastor to visit the members.

They want a pastor to reach out and evangelize in the community.

They want a pastor to do the work for the church.

These situations are almost without hope. The members of the church just want a hired hand, not a pastor. They want someone do the work of ministry for the church. They don't want to change. They don't want to make painful and necessary decisions.

They want a pastor silver bullet.

It never works. Never.

The Money Silver Bullet

I've seen sick and dying churches with a lot of money in the bank. Conversely, I've seen sick and dying churches with almost no money in the bank. There is simply no strong correlation between money in the bank and health of a church.

Still, there are many churches with little money that see additional funds as their silver bullet. The members and leaders typically point to a larger and, presumably, more affluent church as clear evidence that money is the solution. Allow me to provide a cogent example of a church I offered to consult a few years ago.

The pastor of the church had announced his retirement, so some of the leaders contacted our consulting firm, Church Answers, for help. (I could do an entire book on churches that view a consultation as a silver bullet. These churches see the consultation as something an outsider does without the church having to make any changes.)

I agreed to meet with the five elders of the church via a teleconference call. The situation was not atypical. The church had declined eight consecutive years. The pastor, though he had just announced his retirement, had been in a coasting-to-retirement mode for at least three years. Attendance was down. Community impact was negligible. Morale was low. And, of course, money was down. Giving had declined pretty much commensurate with the attendance decline.

As I typically do in initial interviews for a consultation, I asked the leaders what they perceived the problem to be.

The first elder spoke and blamed the situation on the community. "People used to come to our church from the neighborhoods all the time," he said. "They know where we are. I don't understand why they don't come."

That's right. Blame it on the community. I'll get to that issue later in the chapter.

The second elder seemed to be speaking for the rest of the group. "Look," he began, "let's face the facts. We are barely paying our bills and making payroll. We don't have any money. There are two other churches in our town that have all kinds of attractions. They have a huge recreation facility (more on facilities later). They have a student minister and a children's minister. They must have a lot of money to spend on marketing. I could go on and on. The bottom line is, if we had that kind of money, we would be growing too."

I could see on my computer screen the other elders in the room. They were all nodding in agreement.

Lack of money was the problem. More money was the solution.

I tried to encourage the elders by telling them of a church in New England that had only a dozen members and no money. The church prayerfully began to reach a resistant neighborhood with acts of kindness and other ministry opportunities. Though at times painfully slow, after two years, the church has thirty-five in attendance.

I looked at the elders on my computer screen. I was talking to the wall.

They thought money was the silver bullet. I knew I could not help them unless that perspective changed dramatically.

It did not change.

The Music Silver Bullet

"The growing church down the road has contemporary music. If we want to grow, we have to become a contemporary church."

Please hear me clearly. Understanding your community and generational context is critically important. And that context may point the church to a different worship style such as a more contemporary approach.

Frankly, for most churches that point to changes in music style as a silver bullet, the problem is not the music. It is both a lack of awareness of the context and an unwillingness to change. The stuck-in-the-rut music style is more of a symptom than a problem.

At a friend's request, I spoke to a remnant of church members who thought I could be the silver bullet to their decline and likely demise. I can't remember what I said to the group, but I do remember their questions:

- Do we have to do away with hymnals?
- Do we have to have those stupid screens with words on them?
- Do we have to become a rock-and-roll church?
- Do we have to have guitars?
- Do we have to have drums?

The person who asked the question about drums followed up with this statement: "We will have drums over my dead body!" The remnant of church members applauded her.

Somehow these church members had gotten the message that a revived church has a singular approach to music and worship. And they wanted nothing to do with that approach.

The church's problem was their inward focus, not the worship and music issues.

The music and worship style can be the greatest fear of a church needing revitalization. Or it can be perceived as the silver bullet.

The church I visited closed its doors that same year.

The Location Silver Bullet

Most churches don't need a new community. They need to reach the community where they are. For certain, there are a few cases where there is no longer a community, such as a neighborhood that has become totally commercial or industrial. Those situations are rare, and they are definitely the exceptions. Most churches have a community to reach. God gave them their locations. Their addresses are not accidents.

But the scenario is familiar. Many of the members moved out of the community as the area transitioned.

The new residents weren't like the church members. There was little to no interaction between the community members and the church members. After all, they didn't live in the same area.

So the church begins a downward spiral since there are no people coming to worship services from the community. This problem is exacerbated by the painful reality that the church is making no attempts to reach the community.

But your church address is not an accident.

Too many churches think it's the community's fault. The members and leaders think the silver bullet is to relocate. For certain, that can be a reasonable solution if the members are concentrated in another area and if the church can put the church facilities in the hands of people who will reach their community.

The problem is that church relocation is a massive undertaking. Few churches can actually pull it off. Another problem is that the relocating church usually has an inward focus. The new location is not the silver bullet to turn the church into a Great Commission congregation.

Except in rare exceptions, a new location is not a silver bullet.

The Facility Silver Bullet

This silver bullet can be a variation of either the money silver bullet or the location silver bullet.

For some churches, it is "if we build it, they we come." Rarely does this play out like the movie *Field of Dreams*. I've seen countless churches build facilities with a confidence that the community is just waiting for that new worship center or new recreation center. Instead of getting new people in the church, they often get a new debt burden that hinders them from having resources for ministry.

Don't get me wrong. Churches often need to upgrade their facilities. On some occasions, they need to build new facilities. Frankly, I've been in countless churches where the condition of the buildings reflects attitudes of negligence and apathy. These churches definitely need to do something about their facilities.

But please don't see facilities as silver bullets. They never are.

The Anatomy Finding: No Silver Bullets

I love hearing from members and leaders of revived churches. I love hearing their stories of prayerful grit, determination, and obedience. Though their paths are not easy, they have chosen obedience, sacrifice, and service to others.

You know what I never hear? I never hear of the silver bullet that solved their problems, that turned their church around.

I can almost anticipate your question. What about the church that got a new pastor, and that new pastor led the church to an incredible turnaround?

In those churches, the pastor was not seen as the silver bullet, the lone and magical solution to the church's problems. To the contrary, if a pastor leads a healthy revitalization, that pastor is not doing it alone. The church has joined the pastor in that effort. They are working with the pastor. They are doing ministry with pastor. They are praying for the church and the pastor.

Churches that see pastors as silver bullets essentially see them as hired hands. Pastors must visit, evangelize, counsel, go to meetings, solve problems, and, if they have time, prepare sermons. Don't expect the members to do most of that ministry, because that's what they pay the pastor to do.

Our anatomy of revived churches, to the contrary, showed churches where members and leaders stopped making excuses and got down to the nitty gritty work of revitalization. They knew they could not delegate or outsource obedience. And they knew revitalization would not and should not take place with a silver bullet.

Revived churches got it.

There are no silver bullets.

Questions for Prayerful Consideration

1. What is your understanding or definition of silver bullets in churches?
2. Why is the silver bullet concept not aligned with the Great Commission of Matthew 28:19–20 or Acts 1:8?
3. Why do you think the pastor is the most commonly perceived silver bullet for churches?
4. Why is worship or music such a contentious silver bullet in many churches?
5. What should a church do if it wants to abandon the silver bullet mentality?

Chapter 7

Anatomy Finding #7: Choosing Meaningful Membership

We had over fifty deceased people on our membership rolls, fifteen people who were members of other churches, and ten people who were members of two other churches.

And we had only 124 members!

It was my first church. Our attendance was seven until my family joined. I was curious. How could we have 124 members with only seven in regular attendance?

Obviously, I asked the church clerk for the membership records. I then asked the seven attending members to sit down with me while I called out their names. It went something like this:

"Jim Roosevelt?"

"Dead."

"Joanna Chapman?"

"She joined the Presbyterian church twelve years ago."

"Bryan Freeman?"

"Who? Never heard of him."

"Patricia Newman?"

"She's dead too. Lovely funeral. About twenty years ago."

You get the picture. Of our "members," fifty-one were dead. Others had joined one or even two different other churches. Some of them couldn't be found anywhere. A few were unknown to the remaining members.

For certain, we need to clean up our membership rolls. Such artificial and inflated numbers cause many people to question the validity of church membership. But membership is valid. It is biblical.

Do you remember the first time the Bible refers to those identifying with local congregations as "members?" It was in 1 Corinthians 12 where Paul tells the church at Corinth their congregation is analogous to the body of Christ. Every part has a function, whether it is an "eye," an "ear," or "hands." He called these different parts "members." At the conclusion of this incredible illustration, Paul tells the church, "Now you are the body of Christ, and individual *members* of it" (1 Corinthians 12:27, emphasis added).

The point is clear. Membership is not having your name on a roll, though there's nothing wrong with keeping track of people that way. Ultimately, membership is about belonging and contributing. We belong to a local community of believers. And we are expected to be a contributing and serving part of that community.

The "hand" is never told in 1 Corinthians 12 to stop working. The "mouth" is never told to stop speaking. The "feet" are never told to stop going.

Membership has meaning. Membership means sacrificing for the greater good of the body. Membership has clear expectations.

The Quiet Revolution

There has been a membership revolution the past three decades. It has been a quiet revolution with few people either acknowledging it or celebrating it. Tens of thousands of churches around the world have moved from insignificant membership to meaningful membership. The former just adds names to the church roll. The latter makes every effort to bring people into the church with clarity of information and clarity of expectation.

Most of the times we have called these entry points "membership classes" or something similar.

People do not join these churches as they join country clubs. They don't simply pay their dues and get their perks. To the contrary, they give sacrificially and serve sacrificially. Biblical membership turns secular membership on its head. Biblical membership is about giving instead of receiving, serving instead of being served.

In our anatomy of revived churches, we found that almost all these churches became a part of this revolution. A pastor of a church in Missouri told us a story that was common of many of the revived churches.

"One of our problems," he began, "was our feeble attempt to lead a church revitalization with members who had no idea what biblical membership is. They basically saw the church as a place to meet their social and personal needs. I was beating myself up against the wall trying to get them to change."

We asked him to provide some details of the change he began to lead.

"Well," he explained, "I first had to get permission from the existing members to begin a new member class. We had to start teaching biblical membership and giving clear expectations to those joining our church."

We asked the obvious question. Did it work?

"Not at first," he admitted. "The idea of a new member class represented change, and the current members then did not like change. I finally figured out the main problem. They didn't want to be a part of the class themselves. Of course not. Why would they support something that required them to do something different?"

The pastor paused a moment and smiled. "So, I declared all current members 'grandfathered' into membership," he said. "They didn't have to be a part of the class. It would be for new members only. Now, I would have preferred everyone go through the class, but I had to work with what they gave me."

He continued, "Over time, we began to get members who were ready to serve and give. They had a totally different attitude than the 'non-class' members. It caused some tension at times but, after about three years, you feel the tide turning."

Three years? He saw the unspoken question on my face.

"Look," he said, "church revitalization is a long-term process. It is plodding. It rarely happens overnight. I am committed to this church for a lifetime unless God clearly moves me somewhere. Three years is not that long in a lifetime."

To be clear, the anatomy showed almost all the revived churches went from insignificant membership to meaningful membership. And the most common approach was the introduction of a membership class. Let's delve into that process a bit more.

The Three Ingredients of an Effective Membership Class

We began this research journey of revived churches by looking at common factors in their revitalization. But we learned so much more. A good example is what we learned about membership classes.

To be clear, these entry point classes were not always called "membership classes." Many of them had names that weren't so bland. But I won't take the time to delve into the different names; I am more excited for you to hear what was really taking place.

The common theme, of course, was moving the church from low-expectation membership to high-expectation membership. Our anatomy showed, however, different levels of membership classes.

The first level would be simply an *information* membership class. All the revived churches included this level as they instituted membership classes for their churches.

The second level includes *expectations* as part of the entry into the church. We will delve into the nature and depth of the expectations shortly. Almost two-thirds of the revived churches made expectations a part of the membership class.

The third level connects *assimilation* as an actual part of the entry process. In other words, new members are somehow connected with the ministry and/

or groups in the church *before* they are granted full membership. To be clear, only about one in five of the revived churches connected assimilation to the membership class. They are worth noting, however, because these churches reported the best results of all three membership levels.

Noted a pastor from Florida, "We concluded our membership class by requesting the new member to get involved in a ministry immediately. The most common was becoming a part of the welcome team ministry. We are amazed to see how effective assimilation became when we connected it to membership entry."

Now, let's take a deeper dive into each of these approaches to membership entry.

Level One Information

All of the revived churches in our anatomy either instituted new member classes, revived new member classes, or vastly improved new member classes. In other words, one of the consistent changes in the revived churches was a new and focused emphasis on how new members are brought into the church.

All of the membership classes provided information for the prospective new members. Some information was common. Every class included the beliefs or doctrine of the church. Most of the classes introduced some or all of the church staff. If the church was a part of a denomination, it would not be uncommon to share some facts about the denomination.

A significant percentage of the church leaders were emphatic that the information included some expression of vision for the church. John is an executive pastor of a non-denominational church in North Carolina. He has the primary responsibility for new members and assimilation at his church.

"We place a huge emphasis on the vision of the church in the Launch Class," he told us. "We need everyone to know why we are doing what we are doing. It's important for us because our church lost its vision for years. We were just going through the motions, and decline was inevitable. As we went down the tough path of revitalization, we had to make some tough decisions and make some challenging moves. That change and new path ultimately became the vision for our church. We don't want to forget where we have been and where we are going, because we don't ever want to get on cruise control again."

John was clear that communicating vision in the new member class was vital to the health of the church. It was second only to doctrine in importance. Of course, a plethora of items can be included in the new member entry. For the churches in our anatomy, the leaders typically did not try to cram in lots of forgettable information. They either gave them written material or pointed them to information on the church website. A few of the more innovative churches recorded short video courses the new member could complete on his or her own time.

Level Two: Expectation

About two out of three revived churches included expectations as part of their new member entry. It was not unusual to see a church tie the expectations to a vision statement, as Eric Geiger and I demonstrated in our book, *Simple Church.*

For example, a vision statement might be: "Love God. Love Others. Serve Others. Give Abundantly." In this vision statement the members learn that the minimum expectations of them are to attend gathered worship faithfully (Love God); become a part of a small group (Love Others); become involved in some type of ministry (Serve Others); and be a faithful giver (Give Abundantly).

Revived churches did not always use the *Simple Church* type of vision statement to establish expectations, but the greater majority made clear that becoming a part of the church carries both opportunities and responsibilities.

Jennie is director of assimilation at a revived church in Massachusetts. She said adding expectations to the core of the new member class transformed the church. "I can't believe how, after one year, the culture shifted so dramatically in our church," she told us. "It was amazing to see how our church shifted from an entitlement mentality to a serving mentality. We attribute almost all of the change to the way we changed our membership class."

Information is foundational for new member classes. Expectations in new member classes are transformational for churches. But if the church added the third level, assimilation, to the class, the results were nothing less than phenomenal.

Level Three: Assimilation

"A lot of church leaders talk assimilation," Barry shared with us. "But few churches connect assimilation with the new member class. I don't get it. If you begin there, your whole church will change for the better.

Barry is the pastor of a church in Indiana that is getting close to breaking the 200 barrier in worship attendance. The story of the church is amazing. Just five years earlier, the church had twenty-two in attendance and was considering closing its doors.

While there are many factors that would explain the revitalization of this church, Barry insists that tying assimilation to the new member class was one of the biggest factors, second only to prayer.

"When I read your book, *Autopsy of a Deceased Church*," he explained, "I knew we had to change or die. I didn't want our church to become another mortality statistic for autopsied churches. I am excited you are writing about churches that almost died but didn't. That is exactly our story."

Among the many changes the church made was adding a new member class, much to the chagrin of the remnant in the church. "I really had nothing to lose," Barry told us. "They were resistant to any change. At this point, our only other option was to die. So I moved ahead with the new member class and survived the criticisms."

Barry's church was in the distinct minority of revived churches that included all three levels in their new member classes. Only about one in five revived churches moved the new member classes to include information, expectation, and assimilation. But those churches whose classes have all three levels were among the most dramatic turnarounds in our anatomies of revived churches.

So how does assimilation in a new member class work in practice? In its simplest terms, no one is granted membership until he or she is either in a place of ministry or connected to a small group or Sunday school class. In Barry's church, the assimilation facet of the new member class meant the prospective member had to get in a community group *and* become involved in a ministry. "Most of the time," he said, "we asked them to become a part of our welcoming team. That always seem to be a good place to begin. It got them out front greeting both members and guests, and it connected them closely with others on the team."

Barry told us that the new member was asked to serve on the welcome team for six months, but many renewed their commitment beyond that time frame.

The anatomy was clear in its findings. Revived churches were congregations that transformed from almost meaningless membership to highly meaningful membership.

The most common tool used to create a culture of meaningful membership was a new member class. Those entry points almost always included information the prospective member needed to know. They often included the expectations of membership. And though it was relatively rare, some of the most effective churches used the new member class as the beginning point and action step toward assimilation.

Anatomy Complete

For certain, we could share several dozen more indicators and correlations from our anatomy of revived churches. Our purpose in this book, however, was to focus on primary and major factors in church revitalization. These seven clearly stood out more than others.

I have learned, however, that a truly helpful study not only points to the "what" but also to the "how." The seven findings about the anatomy tell us what took place. But we wanted more. We wanted to know how, and even why, the church embarked on the often arduous and never convenient path of revitalization. We will indeed learn "why" it all took place as we conclude the anatomy in the next and final chapter.

Questions for Prayerful Consideration

1. Why are so many church membership rolls inflated and inaccurate?
2. What do these inflated membership rolls say about our churches?
3. What are some elements you believe should be included in the level one, or information part of a new member class?
4. Why would a church include expectations of prospective members in a new member class?
5. Why do relatively few churches use new member classes as a first major step toward assimilation? How would you tie assimilation to a new member class?

Conclusion

Change or Die

Robert was in pain. Alicia was rediscovering joy. Robert was the hurting person at the beginning of the book. His church had closed its doors. It was the church where he had married and where his children had married. Robert did not say the church closed its doors. He said the church died. It was personal. It was painful. Very painful.

Alicia has a different story, a story that is getting better by the day.

"I was a terrible church member," she said abruptly. I don't use the word "abruptly" lightly. Like Robert, Alicia found me at the break of a convention where I was speaking. The moment I stepped down from the platform, she grabbed my arm and spoke her abrupt words.

I've had countless people talk to me, but I've never had someone tell me they were a terrible church member. I had never met Alicia, and those were our words of introduction. My curiosity was piqued.

I did not have to ask a question; she resumed the conversation immediately.

"About six years ago, our church was declining pretty fast," she explained. She spoke rapidly. I could tell she wanted me to hear the complete story before someone else asked to speak with me.

"Our poor pastor was getting treated terribly," she said. I could tell Alicia was a bit emotional as she prepared to continue her words. "And I was one of his worst critics," she said softly. "He was trying to lead us to change. He knew we were in bad shape, probably dying. He just wanted what was best for the church."

I was curious about her obvious change in attitude as well as the change in the church. Alicia was happy to report the rest of the story.

"It began when I was on one of my tirades," she confessed. "It was a Monday morning and I was not happy about some of the changes in the worship service the previous day. I was ready to storm into the pastor's office and let him have it. But . . ." She paused for a moment. "But the door to his office was cracked. Before I opened it, I saw him on his knees facing away from me. He was praying and crying. I heard him ask God to remove him from the church if he was getting in the way of God's work. It broke my heart. It broke me."

I could tell Alicia had a strong personality. She told me about her own personal changes and how she used that personality for good instead of negativity. Alicia became one of the pastor's biggest supporters. She influenced others to join her and make whatever changes the church needed to make.

"More than anything," she shared with me. "I got out of the way so God could do His work and so our godly pastor could lead us. When our church started focusing on others instead of ourselves, the turnaround had already begun."

"When our church started focusing on others instead of ourselves, the turnaround had already begun."

That single sentence speaks volumes. Indeed, if there is a simple summary of these revived churches, that is as good as any.

A few years ago, my research team studied inwardly focused churches. The research of that project complements the work of our anatomy of revived churches. Basically, the older study is the "before," and our anatomy is the "after." Let's look at the ten dominant behavior patterns of the inwardly focused churches and compare them to the revived churches.

Behavior Change #1: Beyond Worship Wars

In the inwardly focused churches, one or more factions of the church wanted the music just the way they like it. Anger and demands for change confronted any deviation. The order of service had to remain constant. Certain instrumentation was required while others were prohibited.

But in the revived churches, the members stopped insisting that certain music styles meet their own preferences and desires. Instead, they asked what was best for the church and how the worship and music might need to change for their context.

"I've actually learned to like some of the new music," Alicia told us. "It's amazing how God can change our desires when we let Him change our hearts."

Behavior Change #2: Beyond Prolonged Meetings

Many of the declining churches in our older study spent an inordinate amount of time in meetings. Most of the meetings dealt with some inconsequential issues, while the Great Commission and the Great Commandment were rarely the topics of discussion. A number of these meetings were contentious and divisive as well.

For certain, the revived church has meetings. But

they are consequential meetings. They are meetings with a clear purpose and agenda. They don't exist to fill a time vacuum. They don't meet just because they are on a calendar.

Meetings in declining churches are routine at best, divisive at worst.

The revived church has moved beyond the unnecessary prolonged meeting.

Behavior Change #3: Beyond Facility Focus

In many of the declining churches, the facilities develop iconic status. It could be a parlor, pews, plaques, windows, and on and on and on. One of the highest priorities in the church is the protection and preservation of rooms, furniture, and other visible parts of the church's building and grounds.

Our anatomy of revived churches revealed a completely different mindset. For sure, the leaders of the churches wanted to be good stewards of well-maintained facilities, but their motives were always different. They saw the buildings and grounds as means for a greater purpose. The declining churches often saw the facilities as an end, not a means.

For the declining churches, the attitudes toward facilities could often be idolatrous. For the revived churches, it was never just about the facilities. The purpose was much greater. You might call it God glorifying.

Behavior Change #4: Beyond Program Driven

Every church has programs, even if they don't admit it. When we start doing a ministry a certain way, it takes on a programmatic status. The problem is not with the programs. The problems develop when the program becomes an end instead of a means to greater ministry. Unhealthy churches cling to programs for the wrong reasons, usually because "that's the way we've always done it."

Our anatomy of revived churches did not discover an anti-program mindset. Many of the revived churches used programs and ministry plans in a healthy way. But the revived churches did not cling to the programs. To the contrary, they began to evaluate all their programs with scrutiny for the right reasons.

And if a program had outlived its usefulness, they had no problem letting it go.

Behavior Change #5: Beyond Inwardly Focused Budgets

Unhealthy churches typically use fewer dollars every year on ministry. Of course, one of the obvious reasons could be a declining budget overall. But, in too many churches, a disproportionate share of the budget is used to meet the needs and comforts of the members instead of reaching beyond the walls of the church.

We found that revived churches tried to find ways to use the budget increasingly for ministry beyond the walls. On an incremental basis, these churches did everything they could to find more ways to fund ministry.

The declining church increasingly looks after the comforts of the members.

The revived church increasingly looks for ways to fund ministry outside the church.

Behavior Change #6: Beyond Inordinate Demands for Pastoral Care

All church members deserve care and concern, especially in times of need and crisis. Problems develop, however, when church members have unreasonable expectations for even minor matters.

Some members expect the pastoral staff to visit them regularly merely because they have membership status.

Our anatomy of revived churches found, however, more members saw their primary roles as doing and providing ministry more than receiving ministry. The members truly believed they were equipped to do the work of ministry. They put the needs of others before their own. While no congregation has 100 percent selfless members, revived churches were clearly moving in this direction.

Behavior Change #7: Beyond Attitudes of Entitlement

This issue could be a catch-all for many of the behaviors listed here. The overall attitude in the unhealthy churches is self-serving, demanding, and entitled. A member of a declining church summed this attitude well: "I've done my time at this church; it's time for people to take care of me." Her "time" sounded more like a prison sentence than church membership.

There were noticeable changes in revived churches. More of the members sought to serve rather than to be served. Instead of "What have you done for me lately?" the attitude was more "How can I serve you today?"

Behavior Change #8: Beyond Anger and Blame

In most unhealthy churches, an unhealthy pattern emerges. As the church declines in health, church members look to blame others for the problems. It typically begins with blaming the pastor or others on staff. Then members blame each other. Some get mad and leave the church. The church declines even more, and the blame and anger are exacerbated.

Our anatomy of revived churches found reversal of these patterns. And just as the negative spiral can feed on itself, the positive patterns can grow as well.

Unhealthy churches have members who get angry and blame others. Revived churches have members who serve and encourage each other.

Behavior Pattern #9: Beyond Evangelistic Apathy

Evangelistic apathy has always been the most pervasive finding in our research on declining and dying churches. Very few members share their faith on a regular basis. Most of the members seemed concerned about their own needs rather than the eternal needs of the world and community in which they live.

I wish our anatomy could report that the revived churches had significant numbers of members sharing the gospel on a regular basis. Unfortunately, that scenario is not even taking place in these healthier churches. For now, we can conclude that revived churches have "a few" members sharing their faith consistently, while declining churches rarely have anyone doing so.

It is our prayer that the few will become many as the churches continue to regain health.

Behavior Pattern #10: Beyond Resistance to Change

If there is a possible summary of the unhealthy churches, it is basically their refusal to make the changes they must make. Their motives may be many, but it boils down to their desire to stuck in their ways of routine, sameness, and comfort. Almost any noticeable changes in the church evoke the ire of many. Sadly, those same passions are not evident in their desires to participate in the work of sharing the gospel to change lives.

It is at this point we could best conclude our anatomy of revived churches. While there is no simple, formulaic answer to church revitalization, this one thing we know for certain. Churches that refuse to change are churches headed toward death. And while receptivity to change does not guarantee a recovery to church health, there will be no church revitalization without a willingness to change.

The choice is simple. Here is the "why" we discovered in the anatomies.

Change or die.

The Choice

We began the report of the anatomy of revived churches with fascinating research from the medical field several years ago. In May 2005 Alan Deutschman wrote a cover story, "Change or Die," for the magazine *Fast Company*. Deutschman expanded his work into a full book by the same title. It was released in early 2007.

As we reported, there were two major reasons the article and the book had such profound reactions. First, his research was unparalleled. Second, the results were shocking. His central thesis reverberated throughout the world. If given a choice between life and death, most people and leaders choose death if they have to make substantive changes.

Now, let's repeat that last sentence in the context of churches. *If given a choice between life and death, most church members and church leaders choose death if they have to make substantive changes in their churches.*

Our churches got away with this self-serving behavior for many decades. The culture outside the church and the culture inside the church were sufficiently similar that change did not seem necessary to reach our communities. Our churches seemed to be enjoying some level of health.

But that perceived health was an illusion. Most churches were doing little more than accommodating cultural Christianity. And when culture began to look dramatically different than the church, most of our congregations did not know how to respond. Instead, they developed an insular and retreating behavior. They wanted to avoid the culture of the world and keep the culture of the church.

But when we avoid culture, we stop reaching our communities. We stop serving the least of these. We stop evangelizing. We stop being the church.

We become a religious country club in full retreat mode.

And then we die.

Our churches die because we have refused to make the necessary changes to see God bring new life through the ministries of our congregations. We do not serve the holy Trinitarian God. We serve the unholy trinity of me, myself, and I.

Anatomy of a Revived Church

So, what is the central thesis of our anatomy of revived churches. In essence, the revived churches chose to live. That choice was arduous. That choice was challenging. That choice was painstakingly slow at times. That choice was almost always painful. That choice required church members and leaders to put God and others before themselves. That choice was sacrificial.

But in the final analysis, that choice was a choice of life.

Here is the complement of "change or die." It is "change and live."

The good news is that we are discovering thousands of churches that are making the decision to live.

The great news is one more church can be added to their number.

That church can be your church.

Questions for Prayerful Consideration

1. How can the study by Alan Deutschman apply to churches?
2. Why do our churches have so much conflict over music and worship style? What is the solution to this conflict?
3. What are the major differences in the budgets of a revived church and an unhealthy church?
4. Why do you think so few church members share the gospel?
5. How have changes in culture caused many of our churches to retreat?

Made in the USA
Coppell, TX
19 March 2020